Four days of Pongal

The Harvest Festival of South India

Written and illustrated by Lakshmi Narayani

To my dearest dad, Late. Shri.R.L Narasimhan

Table of Contents

A note from the author

My daughter's teacher had requested the parents to read books on international festivals to the class. I saw a few other Indian parents had registered for these sessions and assumed that Diwali may be taken already. So, I searched for Pongal books for children on Amazon but my search returned zero results.

As someone who grew up in Chennai, India, I have very fond memories of the Pongal festival. In those days, new clothes were meant only for special occasions and Pongal was one of them. It made us look forward to the festival. The streets filled with colorful kolams, the contests for the best kolam, the pooja and the offering to Sun in the open terrace, the feast that follows, my mom's very sweet sakkarai Pongal, sugarcanes, hearing "happy Pongal" from every known face when you step out of the home, phone calls from near and dear to wish on the Pongal day, the special shows on TV – the list will go on and on.

Here in Atlanta, we do not do much for Pongal. I only make sakkarai Pongal – which my daughters don't eat. So, when I found that there are no children's books on this festival, I felt that my daughters and many other children may not get to know about this fun festival. So, I decided to create a simple book with only the most relevant information on Pongal Festival.

I wanted to dedicate this to my dad because he loved the very sweet sakkarai Pongal and he used to ask me to write on "traditional" topics so that the future generation understood the rituals and their significance. I am sure he is smiling down upon me from the heavens!

Hope you enjoy reading this book to your kids and also help them create their own Pongal memories.

Happy Pongal!

1. What is Pongal?

Pongal is a harvest festival celebrated by the people in the southern part of India that speak the language Tamil.

The history of this festival can be traced back to thousands of years ago. Pongal means "overflowing" but it actually signifies abundance.

A harvest festival is a celebration of the food grown and this is done across the globe during the harvest season. The common features of such festivals regardless of the location include feasts, decoration, prayers, family gathering, and community events.

The people of India celebrate many festivals in the names of several Gods. Pongal is unique as this is not dedicated to any "Gods" but to the nature. It started as a thanksgiving festival during which the farmers thanked the sun, the rain and the cattle after harvesting the crop.

Today, it continues to be celebrated by the Tamil speaking farmers and non-farmers in South India and also by the Tamil-speaking population all over the world.

Harvest Festivals:
Fancy Feasts,
Decorations,
Prayers, Family
gathering,
Community
events...

2. When is Pongal celebrated?

Pongal is celebrated over four days in the month of January, from the 13th to the 16th (these dates will change in a leap year).

January 2017						
SUN	MON	TUE	WED	THU	FRI	SAT
1	2	3	4	5	6	7
8	9	10	11	12	13 Bhogi	14 Surya Pongal
15 Maattu Pongal	16 Kaanum Pongal	17	18	19	20	21
22	23	24	25	26	27	28
29	30	31				

Uttharaayan and Indic Solstice

Pongal marks the beginning of the Sun's yearly journey northwards. This is called "Uttharaayan".

This is also when Indic solstice occurs as the sun enters the zodiac sign Capricorn.

It is celebrated as the Tamil month of "Thai" begins. Hence this festival is also called "Thai Pongal". Thai is considered as the most suitable month to perform weddings. So, after Pongal there will be many wedding bells ringing around the town.

Sun's northward journey, "Thai" month begins, Indic Solstice

3. Why is Pongal Celebrated?

Agriculture has been the main occupation in India. Nature was always worshipped as the invisible force that determined the food supply for the people and also controlled their lifestyle.

The Sun and the rain have always been considered as Gods and people believed that worshipping them will help them have a good harvest.

Thus, they dedicated four days to show thanks to nature and remind themselves about how to nurture nature in order to reap the benefits of the produce on a regular basis.

Before the adoption of automated farming, use of machines and chemicals, people treated the soil and produce gently using mostly their hands for their farming activities. Today, many are going back to natural farming in order to preserve nature.

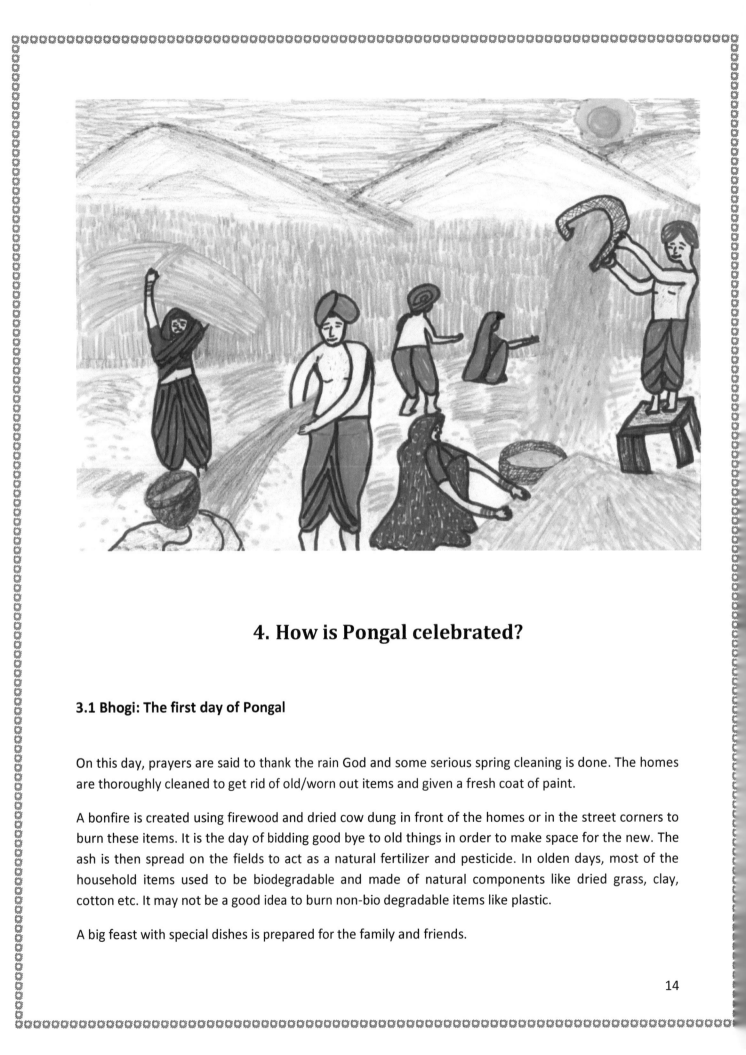

4. How is Pongal celebrated?

3.1 Bhogi: The first day of Pongal

On this day, prayers are said to thank the rain God and some serious spring cleaning is done. The homes are thoroughly cleaned to get rid of old/worn out items and given a fresh coat of paint.

A bonfire is created using firewood and dried cow dung in front of the homes or in the street corners to burn these items. It is the day of bidding good bye to old things in order to make space for the new. The ash is then spread on the fields to act as a natural fertilizer and pesticide. In olden days, most of the household items used to be biodegradable and made of natural components like dried grass, clay, cotton etc. It may not be a good idea to burn non-bio degradable items like plastic.

A big feast with special dishes is prepared for the family and friends.

Bhogi: Clean and Clutter free homes, new beginnings....

3.2 Surya Pongal: The second day of Pongal

This is the main celebration day when everyone thanks Surya – the Sun God, for providing the energy for agriculture.

Everyone dresses up in new clothes and decorates the front of the homes with intricate designs called "Kolam", using special chalk powders in white and other colors.

A special, sweet rice dish called "Sakkarai Pongal" is cooked with rice, milk, lentils and jaggery (typically outdoors using firewood) as an offering to the Sun God. As the milk boils, they let it flow over the pot and the family members holler "Pongalo Pongal" as it flows out.

Today, this dish is mostly cooked indoors on gas/electric stoves, but some families still continue the tradition of calling out "Pongalo Pongal". This is a symbolic way of wishing for abundance.

Sugarcanes are also included in the offering and a big feast is prepared for the family. Sugarcanes are eaten as a dessert – some people prefer pulling the outer shell off with their teeth and chewing on the chunks while others peel off the shell with a knife, cut into small pieces, chew on the sweet chunks and spit out the fiber. Eating sugarcane in this fashion is only for those with strong teeth!

This day is a holiday in the state of Tamilnadu and hence family get together, visits to the older relatives to get their blessings are very common.

Surya Pongal:
Thankfulness,
Feast, Family and
Festivities...

17

3.3 Maattu Pongal: The third day of Pongal

Maattu Pongal is dedicated to thank the bulls that help in plowing the land and the cows that provide milk and various dairy products that are used in day to day life.

On this day, the bulls and cows are washed, decorated with bells and garlands, well-fed and taken around the towns and villages.

A bull taming event called "Jallikattu" and a bullock cart race called "Rekla" used to be held in many villages during Pongal but these events are now banned for the protection of the animals.

Folklore on bulls and agriculture

Shiva – a Hindu God, sent his bull – Basava, to the earth to tell the people of earth to do oil massage every day before bathing and eat food once in a month. But Basava got it mixed up and told everyone that they should eat food everyday and have oil massage once in a month. Shiva got upset with Basava for causing a need for more food on earth and sent him back to help the people of earth to cultivate more food so that they could eat every day!

3.4 Kaanum Pongal: The fourth day of Pongal

Kaanum pongal is the last day of pongal celebrations.

Kaanum means "visiting". In olden days, when travel was not easy, this day was allocated for the families to visit their loved ones. Many used to visit the daughters that may be married in distant places and share the goodies from the harvest. Many folk art forms were performed and people gathered to watch those as well.

Today, people visit their family and friends using more convenient modes of transportation. They also get together at the fairs, beaches, zoos and theme parks.

Kaanum Pongal Today

- *Every year hundreds of thousands of people visit the Marina beach in Chennai, on this day. The second longest beach in the world will seem like an ocean of heads on this day.*

- *Zoos, fairs and theme parks will see record number of visitors.*

- *People from all over the state will travel to visit their relatives or places of interest and hence wading through the traffic will be hard.*

Kaanum Pongal: Family, Friends, Fun places....

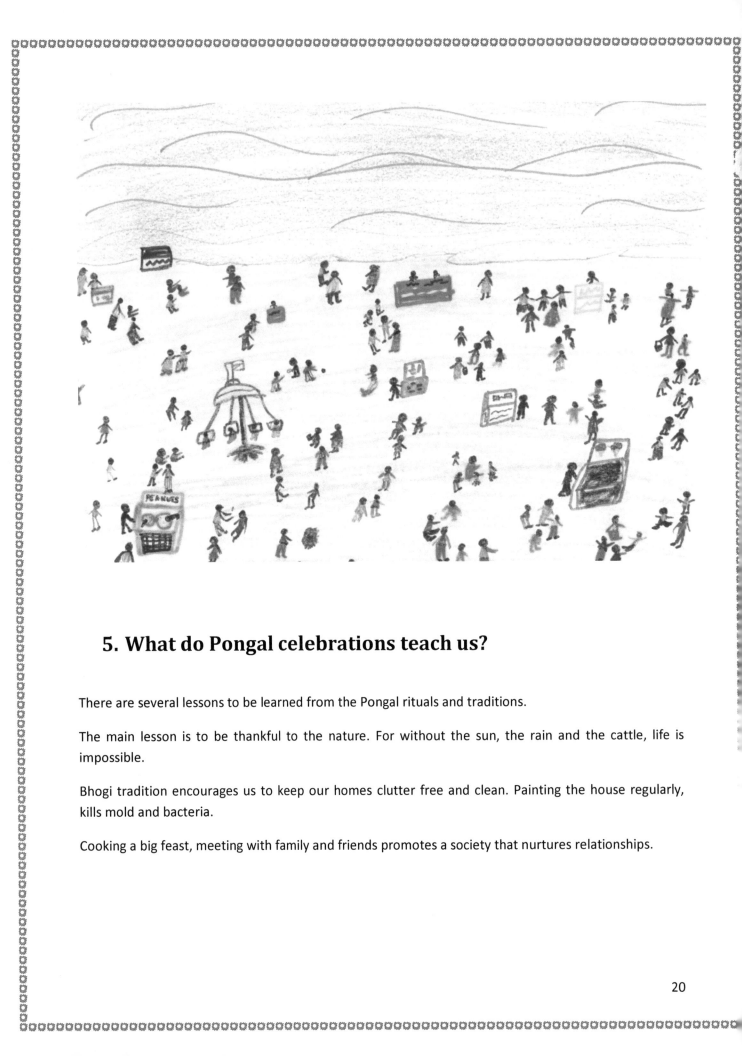

5. What do Pongal celebrations teach us?

There are several lessons to be learned from the Pongal rituals and traditions.

The main lesson is to be thankful to the nature. For without the sun, the rain and the cattle, life is impossible.

Bhogi tradition encourages us to keep our homes clutter free and clean. Painting the house regularly, kills mold and bacteria.

Cooking a big feast, meeting with family and friends promotes a society that nurtures relationships.

Lessons: Being thankful, Cleanliness, nature preservation, society development

6. Glossary

Abundance: A very large quantity of something

Fertilizer: A substance that is added to the soil to improve its fertility.

Intricate: Very complicated or detailed.

Pesticide: A substance used to kill insects and other organisms that are harmful to cultivated plants.

Solstice: The time of the year when the sun reaches the highest or lowest point in the sky at noon. This will result in the longest or shortest days.

Symbolic: Serving as a symbol.

---

7. Pongal Activities: The Quiz

1. What is the name of the day of thanking the Sun?

2. Getting rid of the old things to make space for the new. Which day of Pongal celebrations does this statement apply to?

3. Pongal celebrations go on for:

   a. Two days
   b. Three days
   c. Four days

4. Maattu Pongal is celebrated to thank:

   a. Dogs and cats
   b. Bulls and Cows
   c. Elephants and Tigers

5. What lessons do Pongal celebrations teach us?

8. Pongal Activities: Kolam

Kolam refers to intricate designs created using rice flour, white rock powder or colorful powders - typically drawn in front of the homes in India. In olden days, only rice flour was used to provide food for ants, insects and even little birds. These designs can range from being very simple to very complicated. They are created as geometric shapes or free hand drawings using many different techniques. One can learn to create kolams with some practice. Here is a very simple design that can be practiced on paper and then tried with powder on any floor.

1. Draw two parallel lines of the same length.

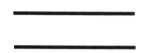

2. Draw one shorter line on top in the middle of the longer lines and another shorter line at the bottom of the same length as the first short line.

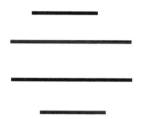

3. Now, draw a slanting line connecting the beginning of the bottom short line to the end of the top long line and another slanting line connecting the beginning of the bottom long line and the end of the top short line as shown below.

4. Draw two slanting lines connecting the short and long lines on the opposite side in a similar manner as shown below.

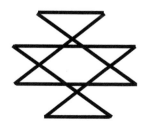

5. Make a tiny circle on the middle of the kolam and you are all done!

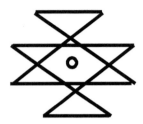

This is the basic design. This can be extended into a large design by making symmetrical improvements and design additions.

8.1 More Kolams: Different Techinques

Two lines at one time technique with color embellishments

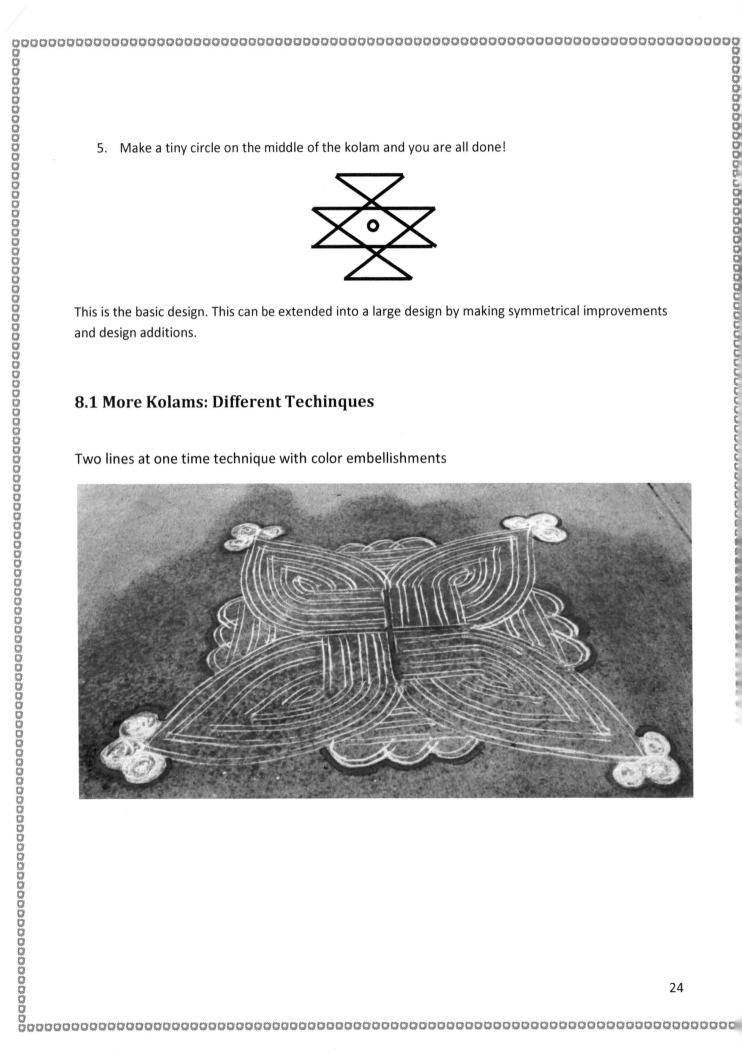

Method

1. Dry roast rice and broken green grams (these will actually be yellow in color) separately until they are slightly hot to touch.
2. Cook both together with 2 cups of milk and one cup of water until they are very soft. This can be done in a thick bottomed pan or in a pressure cooker.
3. Add jaggery and ¼ cup of water in a pan. When the jiggery melts, filter the mixture to get rid of any impurities.
4. Pour this mixture back in a pan, add one tsp of clarified butter and let it simmer for a few minutes.
5. Take a little bit of this in a ladle and pour into a glass of water. When the jiggery mixture does not dissolve, that is the right time to add the cooked rice and lentils to the jaggery mixture.
6. Add cardamom powder and edible camphor.
7. Fry cashews in the remaining clarified butter until they are golden brown and add to the Pongal.
8. Mix well until everything blends together and cook for a few minutes while stirring continuously.

The delicious sakkarai Pongal is now ready! The picture below includes Indian doughnuts called "Vada" – which is also prepared during the festival.

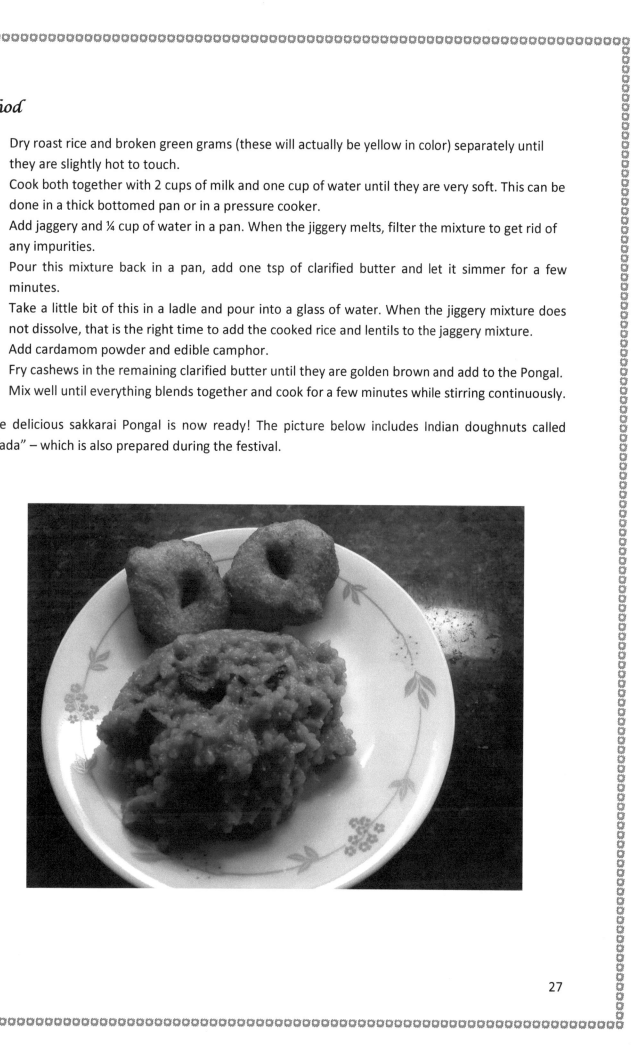

10. Pongal Activities: The Poems

Poem 1:

Pongal is a harvest festival

That celebrates the sun, the rain and the cattle

That reminds people to hail nature and be thankful

That makes every town festive and colorful

This fun festival goes on for four days

When people thank nature in many ways

"Pongalo Pongal" is what everyone says

While seeking God's blessings and grace

Clean homes, family gathering and feasts

Celebrating the harvest and treats

With the festivities and fun, it greets

The warmer weather with celebration and sweets!

Poem 2:

We thank the sun

We thank the rain

We thank the cattle

'Cos its Pongal

Pongalo Pongal, Pongalo Pongal!

We clean our homes, and the surroundings

We meet the family, we meet the friends

We eat the sugarcanes

and sweet sakkarai pongal

Pongalo Pongal, Pongalo Pongal!

Printed in the USA
CPSIA information can be obtained
at www.ICGtesting.com
LVHW071319051023
760031LV00019B/8